The Gift of Compassion

Also by Becca Stevens:

Sanctuary: Unexpected Places Where God Found Me

Hither and Yon: A Travel Guide for the Spiritual Journey

Find Your Way Home: Words from the Street, Wisdom from the Heart

Funeral for a Stranger: Thoughts on Life and Love

Snake Oil: The Art of Healing and Truth-Telling

Walking Bible Study: The Path of Peace

Walking Bible Study: The Path of Justice

Walking Bible Study: The Path of Love

Sisters: Bible Study for Women

The Gift of Compassion

A Guide to Helping Those Who Grieve

Becca Stevens

Abingdon Press

Nashville, Tennessee

THE GIFT OF COMPASSION
A GUIDE TO HELPING THOSE WHO GRIEVE
Copyright © 2012 by Abingdon Press

This book is printed on acid-free paper.

Library of Congress Cataloging-in-Publication Data has been requested.

ISBN 978-1-4267-4234-7

Scripture quotations are from the New Revised Standard Version of the Bible copyright 1989, Division of Christian Education of the National Council of the Churches of Christ in the United States of America. Used by permission. All rights reserved.

12 13 14 15 16 17 18 19 20 21—10 9 8 7 6 5 4 3 2 1
MANUFACTURED IN MEXICO

Keep watch, dear Lord, with those who work,
or watch, or weep this night,
and give your angels charge over those who sleep.
Tend the sick, Lord Christ;
Give rest to the weary, bless the dying, soothe the suffering,
pity the afflicted, shield the joyous;
and all for your love's sake. Amen.

—*The Book of Common Prayer,* p. 124
Evening Prayer, Rite II

CONTENTS

INTRODUCTION

The cost of loving is grief. It is written into the fabric of creation as our temporal bodies kiss the eternal in love. We bear this cost by loving one another with gratitude and walking through the wildernesses of suffering and death with compassion. That is how we live and die as disciples. Bearing the cost of love with open hearts and strong hands sets us on a holy and life-giving path, full of compassion and gratitude. It is a joy to stop in the midst of trying to live out the life of faith to reflect for a moment what it means to offer the gift of compassion. Just typing the words warms my heart. It conjures up in me a ministry that is gentle toward our brothers and sisters and even toward ourselves. It reminds me that just because we are trying to live out lives of faith fearlessly, it doesn't mean that we can't be tender in how we live.

I have been an Episcopal priest for twenty years. I was ordained when I was eight and a half months' pregnant with my first child, so my ministry began with the community I was serving offering me a great deal of compassion. One of my first acts as a minister was to go on maternity leave! Most of the past two decades I have served as chaplain for St. Augustine's Chapel at Vanderbilt University and as the director of Magdalene, a two-year residential program for women who have survived lives of addiction, prostitution, and violence. From my position as chaplain I have gotten to carve out a ministry based on the needs of the people I encounter on the way. This work has been about cultivating a compassionate heart, and I am often brought to my knees in gratitude for my life and faith.

I know so many priests and caregivers who burn out, but there is no law that says people who serve have to burn out. In fact, there are remedies to ensure we don't. Instead we can be filled up by the work. We can find communities to share the journey and spaces that are daily sanctuaries for us. This book is intended as a practical guide and inspiration for those caring for the most vulnerable among us. It's a small book with a big hope that if you are reading it, you know that through your loving acts toward even a single person, you are transforming the world. There is a big, wide community of people offering compassionate care, and my hope is that this writing is another drop in the bucket of tools that some of those caregivers use as they make their way through the valley of green pastures that sometimes feel like a valley of death. I want to share some stories along with prayers, Scriptures, and a bit of theology. Some of the prayers will be handy for you to keep at your fingertips. Some of the dearest Scriptures and oldest prayers read silently or aloud help keep us grounded in our work.

One of the hardest things to do as a caregiver and pastor is to find time to reflect. The work is long and it is tiring. So in order to write this guide, I had to get away from my daily routine. I had to go into the mountains where cell phone reception is limited and distractions are minimal. This past September, after I baptized their baby on a beautiful deck overlooking the Cumberland Plateau, the family said I could use their mountain cabin for a retreat as a gift. It took until the first week of December to find enough days in a row that I could take off and head up the mountain to write. Finally, I got to head into the hills last night. My two colleagues, Susan Sluser and Tim Fudge, came with me to transcribe, cook, and keep me focused on writing. We didn't arrive until late last night, so we just organized the work in order to start writing today. As I went to bed last night, I thought about the daunting task before me. I worried that this time I would not be up for it. That this time, there wouldn't be enough time or resources to meet my obligations.

When we woke up this morning, we discovered that it had snowed all through the night. The whole mountainside and valley were a pure, white painting of peace. It was a beautiful sign, like a rainbow, or a dove in the clouds, that all will be well. There is abundance and peace for a grateful heart. I am grateful that I was given this book to write. I am grateful that I am sitting in front of a beautiful fire with two friends close by, with large windows reminding me that I am surrounded by these peaceful, snow-covered woods, and that I have this day to remember all the mercies and sweet moments of ministry. I don't know who I would be without those experiences. They have given us all we need to make this journey; our task is to share it with others.

Broken

I know it isn't there, but I grab the air
to catch my past and hold it once more.
The feeling of gone is almost too much
for a heart to bear in real time.
I keep breathing because I have no choice,
And I'd rather feel lonely than bitter—
A taste that ruins the finest sunset.
I watch the sinking sun,
that blushes as it kisses the day goodnight,
And marvel at a band of light
Still visible in the shadow of the sunset.
It keeps my almost broken heart beating
To see a glimpse of glory in a darkening sky.
I can let the past go; it is safe in the memory of
God.

—becca stevens

May the meditations of my heart be acceptable and useful to the reader of this book. May you use what is helpful, remember what you need to hear, forget what is unnecessary for you, and forgive me for any offense I have caused. May you find what you need in the following pages. *Amen*.

CHAPTER 1

We Are Worthy to Love
One Another

*But now thus says the L*ORD*,*
he who created you, O Jacob,
he who formed you, O Israel:
Do not fear, for I have redeemed you;
I have called you by name, you are mine.
When you pass through the waters, I will be with you;
and through the rivers, they shall not overwhelm you;
when you walk through fire you shall not be burned,
and the flame shall not consume you.
*For I am the L*ORD *your God,*
the Holy One of Israel, your Savior.
I give Egypt as your ransom,
Ethiopia and Seba in exchange for you.
Because you are precious in my sight,
and honored, and I love you,
I give people in return for you,
nations in exchange for your life.

—*Isaiah 43:1b-4a*

Prayer

Gracious and Compassionate Lord, thank you for the gift of freedom to live fully in the light of your forgiveness. You teach me to love others as I love myself. Give me eyes this day to see myself as your holy child. Thank you for the gift of another day to love you again. Remind me of your gentle spirit and give me the strength to bear my cross this day. Remind me that every person is worthy and deserving of your healing and to uphold the dignity of every human being. *Amen*.

Compassion: A Healing Tool

We can have a compassionate ministry with a ready and loving heart when we remember our place and how we are called to love. There are a myriad of things that make it hard to be present and compassionate for people we are trying to care for. All caregivers carry stories about times when we have felt fearful, self-conscious, angry, rushed, or prideful, which caused us to not be able to be compassionate with people in crisis. Each of those stories teaches us what it means to be present and how grace carries us all through our ministries. The journey is always one of trial and much error, and none of those errors means that we are not worthy of the ministry. Those stories, in fact, lead us deeper into ministries and spaces that ground our faith. For me, all along this twenty-year road, I believe that learning to be compassionate is one of the great healing tools we can carry with us in our vocation. Compassion is a gift to be celebrated and a skill to be honed in the work of chaplaincy.

> "Set me as a seal upon your heart, as a seal upon your arm; for love is strong as death, passion fierce as the grave."
>
> **—Song of Solomon 8:6**

Sixteen years ago I started a ministry called Magdalene that serves women with criminal histories of prostitution, addiction, and trafficking. We have six residential communities where the women live in community and a social enterprise called Thistle Farms that manufactures and sells all natural bath and body care products. The goal is to learn to live and work together and try to love one another without judgment. We strive to keep our focus on healing and mercy. When we worry too much about what others think about us, we trip over ourselves and become too self-conscious to notice the person right in front of us. There have been times when I was so worried or preoccupied that I tried to hide our failures or exaggerate our successes. Especially in the cases of relapse and death, I worried people would think I am incompetent, the program doesn't work, or that we are not worthy of their time or consideration. Over and over the lessons people have preached, in their words and deeds to the community of Magdalene and to me, are that if I am honest and present, people will be kind and love generously. When there is brokenness, people will cry with you.

Compassion Is Not about Me

I don't have to be fearful in how I love people. I do not have to let my fears of inadequacy or judgment get in the way. If I let myself stay guarded, feel inadequate, or feel afraid of what others think of how I am doing my ministry, I am not able to be truly compassionate toward someone else.

One time my family walked into a church in Rome and my son asked me if he could light a candle for his aunt. He was being a healer. For him to heal his aunt all he needed to do, in his six-year-old heart, was to light a candle. To light a candle needed no certificate, no degree in medicine or pastoral care, or no institutional affiliation. For us to be compassionate caregivers, all we need is a heart open to wanting healing for another person. My son loves his aunt and wanted her to be well. She had suffered a horrible injury to her arms and hands in a bus wreck in Cameroon, Africa. Our trip to Rome was after she had endured three or four surgeries, but still had some big obstacles to overcome in her healing.

I loved the act of my son lighting a candle. He got a euro from his dad, walked into a side chapel in the church that was several hundred years old, lit the long match, and then lit a small votive that might burn for an hour or two. Watching him go to the small side altar and light the candle was stirring. It called me to the beautiful, magical thinking of children and my own faith. It stirred in me the wonder of tradition and the hope that lives in all of us for the people we hold dear. It also stirred in me the helpless feeling of being human. No matter what, no matter how hard we work and pray, it may not be enough. It may not be enough or maybe it is more than enough. One candle may be more than enough to cut a path through the darkest hour and lead us to a dawn where we are washed in light. That single act by my sweet child may be more than enough to keep him connected to his aunt forever in an eternal, loving bond. As we left the church, I wanted to hug my son and hold on to him in this state of pure compassion, not mixed with any guile. But he is bound to grow up and carry all the feelings of self-doubt and reality and hesitate to light candles someday. Someday he may wonder what difference this small act of compassion makes and he may forget how it can set a heart on fire.

CHAPTER 2

Calming Our Stormy Seas

And early in the morning he came walking toward them on the lake. But when the disciples saw him walking on the lake, they were terrified, saying, "It is a ghost!" And they cried out in fear. But immediately Jesus spoke to them and said, "Take heart, it is I; do not be afraid." Peter answered him, "Lord, if it is you, command me to come to you on the water." He said, "Come." So Peter got out of the boat, started walking on the water, and came toward Jesus. But when he noticed the strong wind, he became frightened, and beginning to sink, he cried out, "Lord, save me!" Jesus immediately reached out his hand and caught him, saying to him, "You of little faith, why did you doubt?"

—*Matthew 14:25-31*

Prayer

Jesus my shepherd, teach me to walk in the valley without trembling hands and feet. Help me see the signs before me that are your rod and staff leading me to green pastures. Keep me grateful so that I shall not want. Comfort me and anoint my head with oil so that I may dwell in your presence forever. *Amen.*

Compassion Is Timeless

Compassion, like all the gifts of the spirit, is universal in its nature. We feel a timeless love for all people when we feel compassion. Jesus teaches us that compassion can calm the strongest storms we feel. It can remind us that no matter where we are or what circumstances we find ourselves in, love is present with us. I learned a new lesson about this universal and timeless gift of compassion through a recent summer I spent traveling through Kenya, Botswana, Tanzania, and Ghana with my family. Everywhere we traveled there were beautiful robes—cloths of many colors. There were the red ones from the Maasai tribes, the green-dyed patterns from Kenya, the beautiful shimmering cloths made in Dar es Salaam, and the rich colors filling the streets of Ghana. Driving through cities, we saw the robes' colors filling the landscape on busy streets. Even in poor villages that held only memories of roads, where people build their homes out of cow dung, fabulous, beautiful cloth-draped clothes-lines. Every market contained blankets spread out with people selling old, worn, Western clothes. Beside these blankets of grays and browns were yards and yards of beautiful African fabric. People would wear them as skirts, draped over their heads, worn like robes, tied around their necks, in shawls—any way you could imagine. People wear them daily to signify their tribe, their home, their status, and their place in the world. They looked beautiful against the brown, dusty roads in the countryside—this burst of color and these fabulous robes.

We were no different as we traveled. We packed our suitcases with our own cloths that signified who we were and our place in the world. The donning of cloth has always signified beauty, place, wealth, and tribe. In the Bible, Joseph's robe offers us a quintessential story about compassion told in the most dramatic fashion and worthy of a Shakespearean play. Joseph's eleven brothers are jealous and strip him. After many twists and turns in the plot,

Joseph shows compassion on his brothers and gives them each a robe and sends them back to his father to come see him—to be reunited as a family. Later in the Bible, Jesus tells us that when the prodigal comes home (Luke 15:11-32), the father has compassion and runs into the house for a robe to welcome his son home. When soldiers wanted to humiliate Christ, they stripped him of his robes to leave him naked and vulnerable. When the disciples speak of the first convert of faith in Acts, they describe her as a woman, Lydia, who deals in the selling of purple cloth—the cloth that is made into robes for royalty—signifying her place and stature.

"For it was you who formed my inward parts; you knit me together."

—Psalm 139:13

Compassion Clothes Us

The excerpt at the beginning of this section is a story from Matthew that describes Jesus walking on the water in dawn's earliest light in the midst of a storm where fear and ghosts always accompany us. You can imagine the disciples huddled down and bunkered with worry, clutching their robes. "What will happen to us?" they must be wondering. They are trying to brace themselves from apprehension and wonder, cold and rain, when they see a figure walking on the water. Peter gives us a glimpse about how we can let go of all the ties that bind us and move with freedom and compassion toward the work of our Lord. Peter stands up, casts off his robes, and heads into the water—even in the dark, even in the cold, and even with fear and doubt pulling him under. He moves in faith for a beautiful and graceful moment, and we get this idea that is the way to live— to move into that space, unknown, free from everything. That is the space where we are free to love and be present to people, naked and unafraid.

All the things we cling to, symbolically

represented in the clothes we drape over
us, are nothing compared with draping
ourselves with the actual spiritual gifts
that are given to us freely on this path.
On this journey of faith, you can strip the
robe from Joseph, cover it in blood, return it to his father, and Joseph still walks
with God into a journey in spite of being fearful. You can drop the robes and
head out onto unknown waters and it
may be the closest you get to walking on
water with the Lord. Faith holds us up;
it clothes us. It wraps us, and sometimes
we have to quit worrying about it and
working for it and clinging to it to realize
the greater gifts.

The year before my family moved to
Nashville my mother gave my father
a coat for Christmas. We were living in
Connecticut. Now I know nothing of my
father's preaching. I have no memories of
having heard a sermon. I have only heard
stories. My father had an old, worn-out
coat that my mother called embarrass-
ing. They had five small children, and

she decided to give him a fancy coat—a Jacob-gift-to-Joseph-style coat. She said that he could wear it to all the occasions where a priest needs to wear a decent coat. He could wear his old, nasty coat for everything else. So it was that on this particular Christmas, someone came to our home in the evening and knocked on the door. It was a guy riding the rails, and he came and knocked on the rectory door to ask for help and assistance. My mom says we were all gathered in the living room. She heard the door open and then the hall closet door opened. "Oh, no, he's going to give away his old coat, and he'll just have his one, new coat, and it will get ruined," she worried. The front door closed, my father came into the living room, and my mother asked, "Did you give him your old coat?" "No," he said, "I gave him the new one." There was no way my mother could know at the time that my father would not live another winter and had no need for that coat. That coat and giving it away still preaches beautifully forty-three years later.

> "Do not fear, for I have redeemed you; I have called you by name, you are mine."
> —**Isaiah 43:1**

I took a tour of Goodwill Industries' warehouse in Nashville. I walked into a 100,000-square-foot warehouse filled with huge crates of discarded clothing, piled high. It was like a mausoleum for clothes. The Goodwill stores sell more than 50 million dollars' worth of clothes a year, and this was all just the extra. Because there is so much, they end up selling it to a dealer for eighteen cents a pound. Eighteen cents a pound is ultimately what all this stuff we wear on our backs and carry, and pack, and preserve is worth. The guy who buys it for eighteen cents a pound ships it to Africa where it's laid out on fabrics on dusty roads. We can be compassionate, we can be free to love, because of the stuff that we think we are holding onto in the end isn't really the valuable stuff in our lives.

Instead we should strive for faith, not just in theory but in practice, in what we do daily with the material things that we buy and wear and consider worthy.

When Christ enters Jerusalem, people throw their robes on the ground to honor him. When Jesus is stripped and naked on the cross, the soldiers, still not getting it, cast lots just for the undergarment of the robe he wears. Consider the lilies of the field, our Lord tells us. Consider how they neither toil nor spin for those things, yet Solomon in all of his glory, in his beautiful robes, is not arrayed like one of these. Everyone worries about these things that symbolize so much about what we value in this world; but you are different. You know the true value of your life and how beautiful you already are.

We all worry about the things we wear and what we eat. It is called being human. It is when we are graced by faith to cast off those things, even in the midst of dark and stormy nights, that we are graced with a faith full of universal compassion that reaches out to others to love and serve. I am so grateful for all the lessons contained in the Scriptures that teach us to trust that God's presence is the most valuable gift we have been given. Our job in faith is to let go of all the stuff that fills our lives and our minds that prevents us from seeing and feeling that presence. One of the great gifts of offering care and love to others is that God's presence is made more visible to us. It makes it easier for us to let go.

CHAPTER 3

The Call to the Miracle of Compassionate Discipleship

Then the king will say to those at his right hand, "Come, you that are blessed by my Father, inherit the kingdom prepared for you from the foundation of the world; for I was hungry and you gave me food, I was thirsty and you gave me something to drink, I was a stranger and you welcomed me, I was naked and you gave me clothing, I was sick and you took care of me, I was in prison and you visited me." Then the righteous will answer him, "Lord, when was it that we saw you hungry and gave you food, or thirsty and gave you something to drink? And when was it that we saw you a stranger and welcomed you, or naked and gave you clothing? And when was it that we saw you sick or in prison and visited you?" And the king will answer them, "Truly I tell you, just as you did it to one of the least of these who are members of my family, you did it to me."
—Matthew 25:34-40

Prayer

Grant us, gracious Lord, the privilege to offer our best this day for you. Make our hearts big

and our spirits generous. Keep us renewed by
the miracles of love and time so that the more
we offer to you, the more we feel in us. I lift
up my soul to you and put my whole trust in
you. Lead me and teach me every morning how
to love again. Teach me how to cherish life
through every part of creation. *Amen.*

Compassion Is Christlike

Matthew 25 is a benchmark text for
those of us who are trying to live out a
ministry based on compassion offered
to those who are suffering. It is this text
that carries those ministers quickly and
easily to justify their compassion before
others who are more skeptical. This text
preaches that when we act with compassion toward others, we are indeed serving Christ. But it is also a rich theological
statement about what kind of Lord we
are serving.

I have always been so grateful for my
seminarian training at Vanderbilt Divinity School. It has helped me understand
the role of compassion as a model of dis-

cipleship and a deep theological path. The motto at Vanderbilt is "Minister as Theologian," which means they train students in their three years to learn about the language of God. One of the goals is to interpret what it means to believe in God and then go back into the world and preach it in our words and deeds. It is a beautiful motto. Vanderbilt, like many other divinity schools, implements this idea through its academic coursework, requiring students to do some serious biblical exegesis in the Hebrew Bible and New Testament theology. Each student is also required to study systematic theology, church history, and pastoral care, as well as participate in field education. The hope is that through study, work, and prayer, ministers' language and prac-tices become the best possible reflection of God. The goal is to have an image of God that is full and broad, in order to invite as many people as possible to participate in faith communities.

> "You shall go out in joy, and be led back in peace."
>
> —Isaiah 55:12

Imagine if you will that you are walking by a still lake on a quiet fall morning. The lake looks like black glass and when you look into it, you can see a stately grove of maple trees growing just on the opposite side. It's not just that the colorful maple trees are reflected perfectly in the water; it's that there is a certain unique beauty created by the entire image. This brilliant reflection holds the blue sky, the puffiness of the clouds, and the depth of the water. That is how our theology should look—a reflection of God that is stunning in and of itself; that lifts us up to a new place; that opens up new spaces for us.

But truly, how we use theology can be baffling, confusing, and frightening, where the waters are rippled and it is hard to catch a glimpse of God's reflection at all. Theology can be misused to try and explain away horrific catastrophe, heartbreaking events, or history. Theology then becomes confining, as it is translated into closed doctrinal systems that muddy the waters rather than cast a clear reflection. Theology becomes the mortar and bricks used to build walls to separate people. If we don't have right thought, if we don't have right affiliation, or if we don't meet the standards, people close us out or throw us over that wall. And it gets so confusing to me—all the theological language that is heavy-laden. Oftentimes, it seems so much less like a beautiful, colored reflection of God's glory and more like a flat, foreboding image of a cold winter, where I will be left outside. Being left out happens in subtle and really cruel ways. And when I get the most confused, or the most troubled by theological discourse in this world, I have to go back to the beginning, to the most basic theology we know. God is love.

This basic theology means that the first word in our thinking is love. It means that the last word in our theology is love; and that our theology and our language, when we talk about God, it better be imbued in love, so that it runs the course of whatever conversation we're having. If love does not begin and end our theological conversations, they are truly not conversations that reflect our Lord and God. Those other conversations might offer solid church doctrine, deep philosophical thought, or even powerful rhetoric describing our political and socioeconomic systems, but they are not reflections about the compassionate Lord who is described in the Gospels. "God is love" is the basis for everything that we know.

Albert Schweitzer was a brilliant theologian in the early 1900s when a lot of exegetical theology was getting started. Albert and other theologians were examining the Gospels to identify which parts were original, what were redacted and added on later, and which parts really described who Jesus was. Did Jesus really think that the end of times was coming? Was he an eschatological preacher and teacher? Did Jesus understand his role as the Messiah? Was the fact that Jesus was the son of God a secret as Mark suggests, or was it laid out as it is in John's Gospel? The theological field of that time was awash in these debates and theological conversations, and in the midst of it Schweitzer wrote his own book defining his contribution, and then he went to medical school so that he could serve the rest of his life in Equatorial Africa as a doctor. His theology became rooted in the central idea that a theology has to be based on a religion of love and that it has to be freed from any dogma that wants to cling to it. He instead wanted to develop a reverence for life. He wanted to live with compassion for others and see that compassion as being the best reflection of God. The rest of his life is a great testimony to that reverence for life. When he won the Nobel Peace Prize in 1952, he took the gift and built a wing on his hospital to serve lepers. He gave those who were hungry food and medicine. He gave to those who were thirsty as much clean water, without parasites and disease, as he could find.

Compassion Doesn't Need Words

Being compassionate toward others in love is the most powerful theology we can preach. And like St. Francis says, we rarely have to use words to preach it well. When you are caring for those who are suffering, you are loving your Lord. When you are tending the sick, you are worshiping your Lord. When you are comforting the suffering, you are embracing your Lord. All of Jesus' theology that we try to study and live by is in the context of love, as he is meeting people on the way to Jerusalem. This gospel is a gospel about love. This gospel is about how important it is to love one another in real thoughts, in real words, and in real deeds. Christian theology is rooted in compassion and is built by the corporal acts of mercy (to give drink to the thirsty, food to the hungry, and clothes to the naked, to visit the prisoner, tend the sick, comfort the sorrowful, bury the dead) lived out.

The gospel story is always about freeing ourselves and not condemning others. This particular gospel is misinterpreted when it is used to see ourselves as sheep and those that do not engage in ministry like we do as goats. The truth is that we're all goats, and we are all sheep. We actually change places pretty readily; and the call is to come back together and love one another. It's that important.

If compassion is our groundwork for our best theology, how do we learn to be compassionate? In my twenty years of pastoring, I don't think we find compassion in books or programs, in and of themselves. Those things help lead us toward compassion and name the compassion that rises within us, but compassion is really found in the willingness of one person to walk with another through the valley of the shadow of death and the wilderness of suffering. That is compassion in its purest, most unadulterated form. Compassion is felt in the loving action of the person setting aside time to come visit, in a person who is willing to lay aside his or her own fears to be present to another, and in a person opening his or her eyes to behold the beauty of the person he or she is caring for.

Compassion Is Born from Love and Raised on Openness

You cannot fake compassion. When it is there, it is intimate and deep. Compassion is born from love and raised on openness to the world. Humor can feed it, joy can sweeten it, but cynicism will choke it out. Anxiety will make it feel out of reach, and fear tends to make our compassion pretty shallow. The Buddhist prayer of compassion helps us move into a space of compassion in our ministry with ease and grace. The prayer is repeated four times. It is first said for ourselves, then it is said for someone we love, then it is said for someone we think of as our enemy, and then it is said for the world. This version of a prayer comes from Thomas Merton.

> May you be peaceful, happy, and light in body and spirit. May you be free from injury. May you live in safety. May you be free from anxiety and worry. May you learn to look at yourself with the eyes of understanding and love. May you be able to recognize and touch the seeds of joy and happiness in yourself. May you learn to identify and see the sources of anger, craving and delusion in yourself. May you know how to nourish the seeds of joy in yourself every day. May you be able to live fresh, solid, and free. May you be free from attachment and aversion, but not indifferent.

This prayer can help us remember that we are compassionate and loving givers. We are worthy to do this work and we are strong enough for the tasks before us this day.

Compassion Is a Miracle

A theology of compassion is not based on feeling or wishful thinking; it is pure and solid theological work based on central acts such as those demonstrated by Jesus in the Gospels. For me, this means that every day I may not feel like helping the women I work with who are trying to come off the streets. I may not feel like visiting the hospital. I may not even feel like helping my husband, who has just undergone surgery, up the stairs. But every day I remember what love would have me do. Every day I make sure I help my husband up the stairs, and I do the work set out before me, and that means that every day I have gotten to be with my Lord. That feels like a miracle to me.

CHAPTER 4

Do Not Grow Weary in Love

Why do you say, O Jacob,
*   and speak, O Israel,*
"My way is hidden from the LORD,
*   and my right is disregarded by my God"?*
Have you not known? Have you not heard?
The LORD is the everlasting God,
*   the Creator of the ends of the earth.*
He does not faint or grow weary;
*   his understanding is unsearchable.*
He gives power to the faint,
*   and strengthens the powerless.*
Even youths will faint and be weary,
*   and the young will fall exhausted;*
but those who wait for the LORD shall renew their strength,
*   they shall mount up with wings like eagles,*
they shall run and not be weary,
*   they shall walk and not faint.*

—Isaiah 40:27-31

Prayer

Lord, you give strength to the weary and increase in us the ability to love and serve. Keep us faithful in our duties, watchful in the night, and steadfast in our devotion so that we can grow in our ministry as strong as eagles' wings and as consistent as the oceans' tides. You have done great things for your servants, in your embrace alone can we rest. *Amen*.

Compassion Comes from Being Present at a Hundred Deaths

I love this passage from Isaiah. It is a testimony to faith to believe that we can serve one another our whole lives and not grow weary. Sometimes I think that the difference between an old priest and a young priest is a hundred deaths. Sitting by a hundred deathbeds teaches a person that grief and death are not tests on our faith, but are sacred spaces that we walk through together in love and compassion.

Part of what makes us weary is thinking about all the numbers: the time, the money, and the costs of ministering to a hurting world with compassion. There are countless passages in the Scriptures that say we do not have to be weary. We can be hopeful, because we have been promised that the harvest is coming, the burden is light, and the yoke is easy. The only way any of that feels true is by remembering that we are a part of a larger healing community that offers their gifts and talents to the person in need. But our job is not to fix other people. We are only a part of a community of healing, making it much easier to bear the burden of being a real and symbolic presence of the Holy in spaces that can be frightening. To see things as new and to be changed by them, to be open and present allows us not to become wearied.

I remember the first time I walked into a room with an eight-day-old baby who was dying. I walked in afraid and noticed that the nurse was crying. To see a professional in the room with teary eyes for a dying baby made it easier to feel and be present in the room. She reminded me that even though it happens every day, when it happens in your presence, it is heartbreaking. When things are old as the hills and fresh as the new day, there is sacred ground.

> "So let us not grow weary in doing what is right, for we will reap at harvest time, if we do not give up."
>
> **—Galatians 6:9**

It's all about how you look at it. The numbers and tasks can be overwhelming when you forget to see them as cardinal numbers. Cardinal numbers are the numbers we learn about in math. They are numbers that are symbols for other things that we can manipulate to make equations from and draw conclusions by. As caregivers we deal with cardinal numbers in the percentages we are given, the average length of life, and the cost per procedure. They are numbers that we use, but they are emotionally detached from us. The numbers themselves are neutral.

Cardinal numbers are just symbols; they are just things, but there is more to them than that because cardinal numbers can become ordinal. What they symbolize becomes an ordinal number as it takes form with rank and place. All of a sudden, it's not the number four, but fourth. All of a sudden, it's not 15 percent live a year after being diagnosed with this stage of cancer, it's "Please God, let my friend be counted among those few." When we take numbers and put them in context, all of a sudden the reality of where we are and who we are makes more sense. The whole gospel is about ordinal numbers. The stories it tells are relational; they always put us in a particular place and time so that we are engaged, not numbed, by the plot. They don't let us get lost in huge and detached statistics.

Compassion Is about This One and the Next

The gospel is always dealing with the next one—the one ahead of us who challenges our faith. In Matthew 15 we find the story of the Canaanite woman coming to Jesus for help and how she tests the compassionate ministry of Jesus. Like Jesus, we are all tested in just how compassionate we can be. This is the first woman who has an argument with Jesus about healing. You might wonder in a cardinal sense of number, "What is the big deal?" I did the math, and percentage-wise, this woman is less than .013 percent of the people in Matthew who ask for healing. Show her mercy. Let her daughter be healed. Seems like an obvious thing to do. Jesus has fed five thousand with five loaves and two fish. He has visited an entire village of suffering people, and all they just touched the fringe of his coat and were healed. He has helped a man with withered hands and a blind man. Then comes this poor foreign woman, this needy mother with nothing, who wants help. You know what it means. You know what this next one means in the rankings. Everyone knows what it means. If you let it happen for her, it opens up the floodgates, and you have to help everyone. You know it. She is the dam who holds back the river of need in this world. We have to draw the line somewhere, and I'm sorry, the disciples say. Not her too. But he does help her. Because of her faith, he responds in kind.

> "Come to me, all you that are weary and are carrying heavy burdens, and I will give you rest."
>
> **—Matthew 11:28**

There are always two facets of the gospel that exist side by side. There is the particular and the universal. They live together and the numbers get all jumbled in between. This Gospel story puts us face to face with that—the particular and the universal; the first and the last. The Canaanite woman is both of those things and everything in between. Does love have the power to heal that? Are there really that many crumbs under the table? That's what love asks us to face over and over. It is daunting and has consequences for how we live our daily lives. It is the gospel.

There is a prayer of the Canaanite woman in Rite One of the Episcopal liturgy. It is called the Prayer of Humble Access where all of us are reminded of our Canaanite selves. We pray:

> We are not worthy so much as to gather up the crumbs under thy Table. But thou art the same Lord whose property is always to have mercy. Grant us therefore, gracious Lord, so to eat the flesh of thy dear Son Jesus Christ, and to drink his blood, that we may evermore dwell in him, and he in us. (*The Book of Common Prayer,* "Holy Eucharist I")

Compassion Is Trust There Is Enough

While we do not have to get weary or overwhelmed, we do have to trust that there will be enough—enough for those who are suffering and enough for those who love and care for them. Recently I went to visit a woman in hospice care. I brought my oils and my *Book of Common Prayer*. I read two psalms as her mother and sister rubbed her hands and feet with the oil. Then we said the prayer offered at the time of death, as I marked her forehead with the sign of the cross. I prayed as if she were the only person who had ever died or ever will die. I prayed as if it wasn't just a number to add to the statistics of a hospital. This was a faithful and loving daughter, sister, and friend. She was beautiful and it was heartbreaking to watch her die. Directly across from the hospice, sitting on one of the tallest steeples in Nashville on the crux of the cross, was a huge red-tailed hawk looking toward us. It was as though the hawk was offering a benediction and blessing, like an angel of God. The hawk was a reminder that God cares about the whole world, but he also cares about each person, loving each one of them with his whole heart. God has been present at countless deaths, and the heart that can sustain that has to be love itself.

> "And you shall make of these a sacred anointing-oil blended as by the perfumer; it shall be a holy anointing-oil."
>
> **—Exodus 30:25**

CHAPTER 5

Caring in the Eternal Present

Now on that same day two of them were going to a village called Emmaus, about seven miles from Jerusalem, and talking with each other about all these things that had happened. While they were talking and discussing, Jesus himself came near and went with them, but their eyes were kept from recognizing him.

—Luke 24:13-16

Prayer

May God bless you with a restless discomfort about easy answers, half-truths and superficial relationships, so that you may seek truth boldly and love deep within your heart.

May God bless you with holy anger at injustice, oppression, and exploitation of people, so that you may tirelessly work for justice, freedom, and peace among all people.

May God bless you with the gift of tears to shed with those who suffer from pain, rejection, starvation, or the loss of all that they cherish, so that you may reach out your hand to comfort them and transform their pain into joy.

May God bless you with enough foolishness to believe that you really *can* make a difference in this world, so that you are able, with God's grace, to do what others claim cannot be done. *Amen*. (A Franciscan Blessing)

Compassion Is in the Present

Caring for someone requires that we stay in the present moment. We must tend to the needs of the day and not worry too much about what is coming around the bend, or what we have lost or found around the last corner. It is one of the gifts of ministry. We get to live into the eternal present moment. Time is not linear. In the past, time is a flash of thought; in the future, time seems like an impossible destiny that we may never reach. But this day, this hour, this moment, stretches out and lingers as long as we stay focused on it. It doesn't mean we don't reflect or plan, it just means we stay open to the unfolding moment of the present. Especially in a ministry of compassion, we remain open to this person in front of us this day, and allow ourselves to feel the gifts offered to us in it. It is one of the basic lessons of the whole gospel.

> "Because we look not at what can be seen but at what cannot be seen; for what can be seen is temporary, but what cannot be seen is eternal."
>
> **—2 Corinthians 4:18**

Compassion Is "On the Way"

A nice subtitle for the Gospels might be "On the Way." In the Gospel of Luke, the writer begins the mission of Jesus by locating Jesus in a time and place. Luke's Gospel is filled with the encounters that happened to Jesus along the way to Jerusalem. "On the way," so many stories begin. Then Jesus encounters lepers, a blind man, a woman with an issue of blood, and a heavenly host of other hungry and hurting people. "On the way," he taught the disciples how to love with compassion, not judgment. "On the way," he spent three years covering the distance he could have traversed in two weeks between the Jordan River and Jerusalem. "On the way," he spoke the Beatitudes, fed the five thousand, calmed the seas, taught us the parables, and loved the world.

Without "On the Way," we would not understand the meaning of the gospel or what love looks like. What is special about a ministry that unfolds "on the way" is that it can't be planned; it has to unfold. It can't be a policy; it has to be relational as the community of faith is open to what is just around the bend. In a ministry "on the way," vision is not so much a clearly defined target for the future, but sight filled with grace that remembers how love was sufficient on the road so far and so it will be our guide on the road ahead. Our role is to remain open to the twists and turns that will shape it more and more to be what it is, "on the way."

> "Our steps are made firm by the LORD,
> when he delights in our way; though we
> stumble, we shall not fall headlong, for the
> LORD holds us by the hand."
>
> **—Psalm 37:23-24**

There is a Gospel story that tells us about
what happened on the way to Emmaus,
while it is still Easter day for the disciples.
The story (Luke 24:13-35) unfolds that because of their heavy hearts and minds,
these two disciples suffered from blindness
to God. Yet their hearts burned for God.
Cleopas and his companion may have been
preoccupied, thinking they never wanted
to travel this road in the first place, and as
a result didn't recognize that the person
they were longing for was walking beside
them. But "on the way," they celebrated a
Eucharist. In the breaking of the bread and
sharing of the story, they finally see Christ
is with them. "On the way" to somewhere,
we find our faith. Recently a friend of mine
said that he was more of a Good Friday
person than an Easter person. I think that

meant that with all the suffering and heart-
ache, it was easier to identify God in the
suffering than in the proclamation of resur-
rection. I think I understand, but this Gospel reminds us that they are not separate;
we are part of the same road. We grieve
and hope, we die and are born again "on
the way," and when our hearts are burning,
we find Christ on that road.

My brother, who is a Catholic priest
and dean of a seminary, taught me about
this Gospel. When we first started the
9:00 A.M. Sunday service at St. Augustine's Chapel, only two or three people
would show up. As I got ready for the
service one morning, I peeked around
the corner and saw that the only person
in the sanctuary was my brother. I decided to wait for a few more minutes,
praying that someone else might show up
to join us. My brother was born with a wit
only matched by his impatience and in-
telligence. He is also a fairly conservative
theologian. He once refused me Communion when I went to his service. He loves

me, but we are on different paths on the journey. I waited another minute, but no one came. I didn't know if I could preside at the service with just the two of us. Finally, at about 9:08 I walked out and began the service. "The Lord be with you," I said. "And also with you," he replied. "I do not want to do this and I am definitely not preaching," I thought to myself. As the service continued, we each did a reading and shared a story about when we were kids and began to relax. Then, when we started the Eucharistic Prayer, I was completely overwhelmed by the beauty of the act itself. I saw during the breaking of the bread that Christ was present, and so were both our parents, who had been dead for years. My brother and I were simply continuing the Emmaus journey, blind and given sight for a moment. It was one of the sweetest Eucharists I have ever tasted. We were those two disciples walking, wanting to be somewhere else, when a morsel of bread parted the clouds and with our blindness temporarily cured, we could see it—we were right where we needed to be on our faith journey. I am so self-conscious and hurried sometimes that I forget to recognize the burning in my heart that calls me into the presence of God who is staring me in the face.

Sometimes we get it, sometimes we get to glimpse it, and sometimes we miss it. God is love. God is the most beautiful reflection. The most complex in the simplest reflection we can imagine. It's been there from the beginning and passed down from the prophets. It is the gospel in a word. It is a reflection on creation as if on a black, clear lake. It is when we feed and clothe and love one another with everything that we have. It is the calling of the saints, like Schweitzer, who keep us going to believe that we can be better. It is to love without judgment—the most radical love of all that is proclaimed in the gospel over and over. God is love.

An Old Story

On Hemingway's shelf old books sit
Locked in sacred glass to be judged by their covers—
The titles, though, speak volumes
About the way to find our voice.

"On Strange Altars," "Renown," and "The Long
Valley"
all silent testimonies that even teachers
need guides on the lonely path.
An old story leads us through dense woods.

We all cut paths as best we can with
A line or two from an old story book
And a recipe passed down and
Preserved through space and time.
Old knowledge points us toward home.

—becca stevens

CHAPTER 6

A Communion of Compassion

When they had finished breakfast, Jesus said to Simon Peter, "Simon son of John, do you love me more than these?" He said to him, "Yes, Lord; you know that I love you." Jesus said to him, "Feed my lambs." A second time he said to him, "Simon son of John, do you love me?" He said to him, "Yes, Lord; you know that I love you." Jesus said to him, "Tend my sheep." He said to him the third time, "Simon son of John, do you love me?" Peter felt hurt because he said to him the third time, "Do you love me?" And he said to him, "Lord, you know everything; you know that I love you." Jesus said to him, "Feed my sheep. Very truly, I tell you, when you were younger, you used to fasten your own belt and to go wherever you wished. But when you grow old, you will stretch out your hands, and someone else will fasten a belt around you and take you where you do not wish to go." (He said this to indicate the kind of death by which he would glorify God.) After this he said to him, "Follow me."
—John 21:15-19

Prayer

Dwell in this space with me, Heavenly Spirit. Clothe me in compassion. Help me see beyond

51

this fog. Help me hear more than the babble of my own voice. Help me feel deeper than the brokenness of my own heart, so that in bright light and silence I feel your loving embrace. *Amen.*

Compassion Feeds the Sheep

At the end of the Gospel of John, all the doubts, all the drama, everything has been laid aside. Jesus has been raised and appeared to many of his followers. Yet there is some unfinished business with Peter. Peter is wondering where to go, what to do, and he is in the company of some of the other disciples. They've gone back to what they knew before, fishing, something safe and secure. And there is Jesus, who has come before them, fixing breakfast on the shore. After a hearty meal, the others know that Peter and Jesus have some talking to do, so they fade into the background. Then Jesus asks, "Peter, do you love me?" "Yes, Lord, I love you." "Peter, do you love me." "Yes, Lord, you know that I love you." And again Jesus asks him until it breaks his heart, "Do you love me?"

> "I myself will search for my sheep, and will seek them out."
>
> **—Ezekiel 34:11**

Do we love you, Lord? Then we feed the sheep. This Gospel, this call, is about love, not just loving like a brother or sister, but unselfishly with the deep resources of God. When we don't know where to go or what to do, our Lord comes and finds us in his great compassion. Remembering what failures we have had, what ditches we have crawled out of to stand in this role, is a gift allowing us to offer true compassion.

Compassion Heals the Caregiver

We heal others with compassion as we, ourselves, are healed. It is our best hope that having known healing and grace ourselves, enables us to offer healing to another. We all share a common cup of compassion that is borne in knowing the pain of suffering. All of our histories hold powerful stories of brokenness that can give us a heart ready for compassion. The truth is that I have a heart for women on the streets not because I am so saintly, but because many of the women share that same brokenness I carry. It is critical when we are trying to be compassionate to others and feed the sheep to also be about our own healing, so we can serve others in an authentic and meaningful way. It is an infinitesimal line that separates what keeps us from being compassionate and what leads us more deeply into our own ministry. I cannot let my own fears and worries get in the way of seeing the suffering of others before me. I have to set those aside so I can really be there for someone else.

I think I've been to prison about six times this year to visit folks—many of whom are associated with my congregation and with the community of Magdalene. On one of my visits, in the corner of a visitation room sat a young man wearing a yellow polo shirt with the emblem of a cross on it. He was sitting there waiting, and finally another young man in prison blue came out. I was thinking about the stark contrast about how, if you worry about sheep and goats and judgment, that is not a good place to sit—to feel like the barriers are built so strong and there is no permeation between them. I was thinking about how in that system of judgment, it is really scary and we are really vulnerable. The two young men sat down across from each other, they opened up a Bible, and began to study. You can imagine how that conversation might have gone— about assurance, or pardon, or worry, or all of those things. I go into my meeting, come back out thirty minutes later, look across the visitation room and see the two young men's arms are stretched across the table holding hands and their eyes are closed as they are bowed in prayer. God is here in the midst of the prisoner and the free bent over in prayer together.

"Be strong and bold; have no fear or dread of them, because it is the LORD your God who goes with you; he will not fail you or forsake you."

—Deuteronomy 31:6

We can't let anything get in our way of being able to feed one another, the sheep of God's fold. We can't let our fear, ego, anger, shame, or pride, keep us from being willing to feed others and love the Lord. All of those feelings just cause us to not be fully present and compassionate with people. The journey of Peter, and each of us who is trying to care for others, is one of trial and much error. It's also a journey of exploration and freedom that should lead us into spaces that ground our faith.

Compassion Is without Judgment

The goal of much of the work I do is to learn to live and work together and try to love one another without judgment. That is a hard task. All of us in the communities of Thistle Farms, St. Augustine's, and Magdalene try to work hard to be about healing, to be about mercy. The hard part for me as the chaplain of these communities is to trust that others won't judge us. In those times, it's hard to have the conversation with my God—God, who I love with all my heart and want forgiveness from to keep doing the work. It is in trusting in the forgiveness of a loving God that frees me to love. I can't worry so much about what I have or haven't done. I can only worry about what it is that I can still do to be a loving presence. If I don't forgive myself, or feel forgiveness, I am not open to the healing presence of God.

> "Mary Magdalene went and announced to the disciples, 'I have seen the Lord.' "
> —John 20:18

Compassion Is Communing with God

The other main reason that I am drawn back to the beautiful conversation between

Peter and Jesus is it helps me check my ego. Not too long ago a fellow who was in seminary with me asked, "Are you still a chaplain?" It was a throwaway line, but it struck a chord in me. Chaplaincy is humbling and good work, but I wonder every now and then if I should have done something bigger. To be a chaplain is an artful path of discipleship, but in the church hierarchy, working in institutions like hospitals, prisons, and churches is not perceived to be high in the ranking. Sometimes I have to confront this feeling so my ego won't trip me up as I try to feed sheep with the same bit of grace Jesus has shown me.

When I commune with Jesus, he provides the meal but more important, he provides himself. For me, that sums up what a ministry of compassion is.

"You will not fear the terror of the night, or the arrow that flies by day."

—Psalm 91:5

CHAPTER 7

Jesus Wept for Lazarus

When Jesus saw her weeping, and the Jews who came with her also weeping, he was greatly disturbed in spirit and deeply moved. He said, "Where have you laid him?" They said to him, "Lord, come and see." Jesus began to weep.

—John 11:33-35

Prayer

Lord, open my heart so that I can speak a word of love. Turn my stone into flesh, even though it may cause me pain and I may weep. Let your compassion run deep. Let me feel love this day. Lord, even in the midst of suffering and loss let us keep our hearts and minds open, searching the horizon for a sign. Let our pity and compassion move us to action this day. Let us cry to you and know that you see our tears as precious.

Compassion Is Boundless

I think one of the keys to compassionate care is to keep erasing the lines we
have drawn in our lives. Healing rarely
happens within the bounds of services
or in convenient bites. It comes in waves
as we let go, as we are surprised, as we
come to terms, as we dream, as we stum-
ble onto something, or even as we weep.
It is helpful when we offer care to remember the lines during times of suffering are
so blurry they almost cease to exist. They
are like fragile lines in the sand that are
completely washed away by a sweeping
tide. Healing in these times happens as
we stir soup for our sick friend, as we offer a silent prayer going up the elevator
to visit a relative in hospice, and as we
reach out even when we have no words
left. Compassion requires us not to think
of ministry as offering magical cures,
but deep healing that understands the
mystery of how we are all healed on the
journey.

> "As he came near and saw the city, he wept over it."
>
> **—Luke 19:41**

I attended the funeral of a graduate of Magdalene this winter. I met her a decade ago and feel like our relationship went through many transitions. I first knew her as a woman coming to seek help from homelessness, depression, addiction, and abuse. A couple of years later I knew her as an employee and rescuer of dogs. A couple of years later I knew her as a patient who was hospitalized for liver failure. In all those various roles, it was her soft heart, her quick sense of humor, and her willingness to forgive herself and others that stood out. Her very presence was healing and as our relationship kept changing, it was important to keep being willing to be present to her as we both evolved. At her funeral I told a few stories I remembered and I marveled at the huge gathering in her honor. As well as I knew her, I knew just a small part of her. I didn't know her as a loyal family member, as a fellow church member, or old high school friend. I wept at her service partly because there were so many people weeping for her. She was beloved by a whole community and she was a healing presence for people. I am glad that our lines blurred and our relationship evolved. It was healing for me too.

There are ways of offering our ministry of caring for others that actually promote compassion and get us set in the right direction to walk toward love. What I love about the story of Jesus weeping at the grave of Lazarus is that it gives us permission to listen with new ears to old problems. All along the way Jesus is helping people who are critically ill and who are suffering. It is never recorded that he weeps as he walks. It is when he encounters Martha and Mary, however, as they grieve Lazarus that the Bible says, "Jesus weeps." When people suffer, it is heartbreaking to those who love them. But it is truly hard to work day in and day out with those we don't know or don't love and treat them with compassion and be with them through some of the lowest valleys carved into the body of the earth.

When I encounter suffering and think, "I've heard this story before," I'm in trouble, because I've already slotted the situation and positioned that particular story on the shelf of similar stories. This is not to say that noticing patterns is necessarily a bad thing, but to offer the proper pastoral response I also need to see the uniqueness of this particular suffering. For us to be present in a story, it needs to be heard as entirely new, in all its difference. In the thousand stories I have heard of women coming off the streets, there is something different in each one. The trauma of childhood may be similar, the way the universal issues of violence are borne on individual backs may be familiar, the chaos of addiction might hold a similar pattern, but the difference is in the details. The difference is *the person* telling the story whom I have never met before. She tells her story and says something I have never heard even in the oldest story in the world. It never ceases to amaze me that if I am present, I will learn something in the healing that takes place as the story is offered. It never ceases to amaze me how many times my eyes well up and I find myself moved by the story and the suffering that people endure.

> "I am like an evergreen cypress; your faithfulness comes from me."
>
> —Hosea 14:8

Compassion Finds New Truth

Finding new truth in old stories is important in order to be compassionate. Even Levite priests heard these same stories: a daughter is sold; she is still paying the price; and she is coming back with issues of hurt, shame, betrayal, and anger. But I have never met *this* woman before who is telling *this* story of *this* alley. All of a sudden the story is new and we can be changed by it. We are not called to transform the world; we are called to love it. And in order to love it, sometimes we have to change ourselves so that we can love it more deeply. When we walk into a room, we must be open to whatever conversation will arise and the fact that we may be changed by that conversation as well.

When I first opened the doors of Magdalene, I felt like a chaplain offering an outreach. I had no idea that the women would change my faith and be the place where I learned my best theology and ideas about healing. I thought I would bring my faith into that space, which I think I did in many ways. I didn't know how dramatically the work gave me faith. I remember when we opened the house we built from the ground up. It was tons of work, and I kind of felt like I owned part of it. I went over to the house not too long after we opened and Grace greeted me at the door. "Welcome," she said, "Can I get you some tea?" It made me teary at the realization that it wasn't my house. I was a guest, and I needed to let go and accept Grace's offer. She was the giver, and I was the receiver.

Jesus always knew that healing was coming, but that did not make his journey any easier. For all of us in our work, trusting that healing will come allows us to be brave enough to be present for someone dying. It is a huge task to believe that healing is coming every day. To believe healing is coming is to remember that healing and cure are not synonymous. We trust that our journey begins with God and ends with God, that we are making this journey together and that healing is happening all along the way. We want to be present for however that healing happens, whether in saying prayers, laying on of hands, offering organ donation for new life, gathering family at the bedside, or holding silence.

> "But if we hope for what we do not see, we
> wait for it with patience."
>
> **—Romans 8:25**

Part of our job is to illuminate that healing by holding it up to the light for people, because sometimes it is hard to see. We have no idea how desperately people need our gifts, how our presence helps just by showing up and saying that we are here for you. The longer we are gifted to do this work, the better we become at offering the presence of healing. We can enter a life for a moment and bring with us a rich history of knowing that no matter what, healing will carry us through to the next new day. In the end, healing comes even as we pray,

> May your rest be this day in peace, and
> your dwelling place in the Paradise of
> God. May [your] soul and the souls
> of all the departed, through the mercy
> of God, rest in peace. (*The Book of
> Common Prayer*, "A Commendation

at the Time of Death" and "A Commendatory Prayer")

My hope is that when I am dying, someone will offer this prayer over me and believe healing is present. I hope someone will anoint my body with rich oils, let my organs be donated, and let my body be buried according to tradition that all will see this as the best healing I could hope for.

CHAPTER 8

The Last Supper

When the hour came, he took his place at the table, and the apostles with him. He said to them, 'I have eagerly desired to eat this Passover with you before I suffer; Then he took a loaf of bread, and when he had given thanks, he broke it and gave it to them, saying, "This is my body, which is given for you. Do this in remembrance of me." And he did the same with the cup after supper, saying, "This cup that is poured out for you is the new covenant in my blood."

—Luke 22:14, 15, 19, 20 ·

Prayer

Loving God, we thank you for making us one body and one spirit. Help us always to remember that we are in your hands, your feet, and your eyes. Teach us to use our hands to heal, our feet to serve, and our eyes to see you in all that we do. For the sake of Jesus, who offered his body for the whole world. *Amen*.

Compassion Is Sacred Space

There is a space between inspiration and action. It is a sacred time that is almost imperceptible, and where so much hangs in the balance. It is where compassion compels us to move forward and where weariness whispers to go back. It is where our Lord's Supper feeds us. One version of the Eucharistic Prayer says:

> Deliver us from the presumption of coming to this table for solace only and not for strength, for pardon only and not for renewal. Let the grace of this Holy Communion make us one body, one spirit in Christ, that we may worthily serve the world in his name. (*The Book of Common Prayer,* "Eucharistic Prayer C")

We pray for strength and renewal to keep loving this world. It is through eating one more bite and taking one more sip that we believe that prayer is answered.

I went to the hospital to visit an eighty-year-old woman whom I had never met. She requested that I come and give her Communion, the Eucharist. When I walked into her room, she was lying down and thanked me for coming. She told me that she was having risky surgery the next morning to try and clear out her lungs, and that to prepare, she needed to take Communion. I asked her how many times she had taken Communion. "More often than not," was her answer. She then explained that she had been the wife of an Episcopal priest for fifty-two years before his death a few years back. So we started the ritual for the umpteenth time, neither of us using the prayer book. When I concluded with, "Let us bless the Lord," she responded, "Thanks be to God." Then she added, "Okay, I'm good to go." It was the perfect benediction. With the Lord's Supper, we are good to go. It is enough to give us solace, strength, pardon, and renewal. It should be our weekly bread. It will continue to nurture a compassionate spirit and a caregiver's heart.

> "As a mother comforts her child, so I will comfort you; you shall be comforted in Jerusalem."
>
> —Isaiah 66:13

We have been consecrating small Eucharistic kits from the altar at my church that people then take to those who are suffering. I love the kits. They are like toy Communion sets; everything miniature, beautiful, and delicate. Being toy-like doesn't mean that giving and receiving is frivolous, but it does speak to God's enjoyment of us taking part in him. It feels intimate to share Communion in this way and literally have two or three people gathered in God's name and have the Lord in the midst. Keeping the Lord's Supper on a regular basis is essential in a ministry of service and compassion.

There is no better example of the Eucharistic feast than the story of the feeding of the five thousand. It was central to the early church for us to hear it over and over and over again; to take it in and emulate it. Once while I was visiting the Serengeti National Park, which is a wonderful place about the size of Massachusetts, with no electricity anywhere and no paved roads—just dirt paths through it—we were at a lodge and I ordered coffee. They brought me a small teacup of coffee on a tray with a tiny spoon, a pack of sugar, and a little milk to go with it. There was no hope of a larger pot for free refills in sight. There was no one else coming by. That was my coffee for the day. I drank it and left a little disappointed. The next day I got up early as the sun was rising, went down, and ordered coffee. This time I knew that this small teacup of coffee was my allotment for the day. I drank it differently. I sipped it, and I savored it, and I contemplated it. I contemplated how they got this coffee there in the first place. I gave thanks for the generator and for whoever it was who managed to get up early to get out to the lodge to make the coffee. I imagined all the workers making coffee on these harsh landscapes. It was the small quantity of coffee that enhanced the quality for me. I loved it, and it was all the coffee I needed. By the third and fourth day, I was celebrating it. I am grateful that Communion is just a taste of bread and wine. It is all we need and more than enough to change our lives.

In Ghana, we met a new group of friends who are working with some of the sixty thousand orphans in that country. Young women, ages fourteen to seventeen, having babies on the streets, come in to take refuge. This community has formed a women's enterprise to make products, and we met with them one afternoon so that Thistle Farms could start purchasing bracelets from them to include in our product line. With their babies, the girls modeled all the products for us, and then set out a lunch. My family and I sat down, and although the conditions of the kitchen were questionable, we ate some of the food, but left most of it. When we got up from the table, all the young mothers rushed to our food and started eating. How desperate the need is right under the surface. It is scary, and makes us feel like we have to guard ourselves from this kind of need. But in our Eucharist, all the scales are measured differently. On a Eucharistic scale, poverty is when we are sad and fearful in the face of unvanquished and immeasurable joy and love offered in the feast. When we forget the point of the Eucharistic feast, it's time for us to run to the hillside and learn the lessons again about what is quantity and quality in the face of love. On most of the scales in this world, we have resources to offer. We remember it is our task in faith that when we go to the hillside, if we have a loaf of bread, we offer it up. As ridiculous and inadequate as that sounds, that is our job in this world.

> "Come, let us go up to the mountain of the LORD, to the house of the God of Jacob; that he may teach us his ways and that we may walk in his paths."
>
> **—Micah 4:2**

We make our meager offerings to one another and trust that in the giving, it will be blessed. The Eucharist teaches to believe that our Lord, who loves the world with all his heart, will bless it and make it enough. Our Lord, who sees our great need, will make sure that we are invited to share the feast. Our Lord breaks the bread we offer and offers us a piece back that fills us with immeasurable gratitude. It is truly a miracle to me, no matter how many times I participate in it.

Compassion Comes Round Right

Every Eucharistic feast is a miracle. If we did not have this great thanksgiving and feast, we would have to start all over. With it, we have the tools we need to open up a ritual of feeding our bodies, minds, and spirits. The Lord's Supper is what we do to remember. It helps us remember who we are. We are the people of God. We are disciples gathered in a community and coming as equals to seek mercy. We are a living memorial to God's love for all people. Remembering all of this helps us to live out the words of the old Shaker hymn that when we remember who we are, we find ourselves in the valley of delight. We keep breaking the bread and sharing the wine until "we come round right." But the Lord's Supper is also a time to celebrate what God does for us in Christ Jesus. The remembering takes us back, but the celebration moves us into the future where God's love will ultimately triumph.

> "I am grateful to Christ Jesus our Lord, who has strengthened me, because he judged me faithful and appointed me to his service."
> **—1 Timothy 1:12**

The Lord's Supper makes it possible for me to find home anywhere I go in the whole wide world. On several occasions over the past few years, whether I was in a small village in Africa or a city in South America, it was a joy to wake up on a Sunday morning, walk into a church, and begin to participate in the ritual, even without understanding what it was they were saying. Walking up to that table and finding out there is enough for even me is a miracle every time. It is like finding out that even in the midst of five thousand hungry brothers and sisters, our Lord has not forgotten our great need. It is a universal cup of life we share. It is the mostly earthly thing to do, to eat and drink, and it is the closest to heaven I have ever tasted.

CHAPTER 9

Cultivating a Servant Heart

Then Moses went up from the plains of Moab to Mount Nebo, to the top of Pisgah, which is opposite Jericho, and the LORD showed him the whole land: Gilead as far as Dan, all Naphtali, the land of Ephraim and Manasseh, all the land of Judah as far as the Western Sea, the Negeb, and the Plain—that is, the valley of Jericho, the city of palm trees—as far as Zoar. The LORD said to him, "This is the land of which I swore to Abraham, to Isaac, and to Jacob, saying, "I will give it to your descendants"; I have let you see it with your eyes, but you shall not cross over there." Then Moses, the servant of the LORD, died there in the land of Moab, at the LORD's command.

—Deuteronomy 34:1-5

Prayer

Be present, O merciful God, and protect us through the hours of this night, so that we who are wearied by the changes and chances of this life may rest in your eternal changelessness; through Jesus Christ our Lord. *Amen*. (*The Book of Common Prayer*, p. 133)

Compassion Is Servant Leadership

Moses' life and ministry teaches us volumes about the meaning of compassion in our caregiving. After serving God faithfully, God gives Moses a glimpse of the land of milk and honey. He takes Moses up to a beautiful vista and shows Moses the place he has imagined and worked for. And then God says, "You can't go; you have to lie down and die in the land of Moab in the desert." Moses is the one who had an up-close glimpse of God, who went up to Mount Sinai and received the Ten Commandments, and who never lost his faith. Moses was obedient to the end, because after the words from the Lord, Moses lies down in this quintessential act of servant leadership— the Magnificat of discipleship. It is the testimony to what true surrender to love looks like. It appears as if everything he's been about and even his vision will die as well. Yet what he lived for lives on in another.

So God then says to Joshua, Moses'
successor, "I'm going to put the mantle
on you, and you are going to carry it."
And just like Moses did when he parted
the Red Sea, God says to Joshua that he
is going to lead the people across the Jordan River, and it is going to be dry. "You
are going to carry these laws of love with
you—to love God with all your mind,
heart, and spirit, and body, and strength,
and being and to love everyone as you
love yourself, to love every person you
come in contact with as if it is yourself."
And Joshua does it. Can you imagine the
weight of that mantle—of Moses' mantle—to carry that while leading God's
people?

Compassion Belongs to Community

In the last few chapters of Matthew's
Gospel, Jesus is in the seat of power for
religious life in Jerusalem, in the temple
facing the religious authorities of his day
as they quiz him. He doesn't reinvent

love; he simply picks up the mantle of Moses and Joshua and offers it to the people. He picks up the Law of Moses and proclaims that these are the greatest laws, and he repeats the laws that have been etched on the hearts of the children and the children's children. He says nothing in these laws needs to change; these are the laws of love given to us by our Creator. Our role is to buy into and live into them. But God doesn't appoint another prophet to carry the mantle in the same way Moses and Joshua did. Instead he hands it over to the community and says these are the laws to follow. Following God cannot be about authority and lofty ideas and big phylacteries and long fringes. This is not what God's Law, the law of love, is about. It is a prophetic voice that can move outside the church and the structures as we know them. It is humble, and in that humility there is an exaltation that is beyond belief. And he takes the mantle, and he gives it to us, the disciples, to carry the banner of the laws of love, to let that love for us that we have for one another be sealed upon our hearts, a mantle upon our shoulders, and a crown upon our heads.

> "For he is our peace; in his flesh he has made both groups into one and has broken down the dividing wall, that is, the hostility between us."
>
> **—Ephesians 2:14**

I carried these lofty thoughts and ideas into the woods as I was contemplating all the work ahead of me—writing this book, all the fund-raising I have to do, the needs of my kids, a wedding coming up, and laundry—that huge mountain of need that never stops. I was walking in the best cathedral there is—the cathedral of trees in Tennessee where it looks like stained glass of yellow, orange, and brilliant red. I was thinking and daydreaming as I was wandering when I realized that I had wandered into a rafter of turkeys. It was a huge grouping of turkeys, and I was in the middle of it. It was scary. They are awe inspiring, and they are much bigger than you think when they still have their heads and feet. I stood there and wondered what this sign was. Turkeys are all about community and harvest and shared blessing. In the Native American tradition, the turkey is referred to as the earth eagle. It is the humble eagle—the one that is about blessing in a way that is humble but that is also powerful and awe inspiring. It is a meaningful symbol for what it means to carry this banner—not high and proud but in community and grounded. This is the space, and this is our mantle.

Compassion's Banner Is Love

We are the descendants of Jesus, of Joshua, and of Moses. They have given us the mantle of love to carry that is strong enough to bear all. Our banner is love. Our mantle is love; and every action, everything we do, every way that we spend our money, every way that we vote, every way that we eat our food, every way that we love one another, is part of that. We all keep changing to live into it more. We carry the mantle of Moses. That is a powerful movement—to carry the mantle of Moses. It means that we are not carrying the mantle as if we are fighting a battle that we will win for love. It means that we surrender to the laws of love so completely that we tap into the deepest and most powerful source in the world. We love the world, and we are changed by it, and we move in it and change it. It means that we don't talk about love in some abstract, lofty, or romantic way. You don't fall into love; you stand in the midst of it wherever you are, and you bathe in it, and you swear that you will live into love for the rest of your life. This is the movement of which we are a part. It is older and deeper than anything we know. Let us walk in love, please, Lord. Let us humble ourselves and know the exaltation of love itself. Let us be in community and go into the world changed so we can love it better.

Our acts of loving compassion spread in a wonderfully exponential mystery. It ripples through waters of prayer, reverberates through air waves of hope, and dances around the edges of time. Loving and serving another changes the way the whole world lives. Saint Teresa reminds us of this truth when she says every small act of love changes the balance of love in the world. Our compassion inspires others to live with more compassion. I recently received a whole stack of letters from high school students in Hawaii. The sweet letters said that the servant work of Magdalene has inspired them to live with more compassion. One student said that it was a reminder that "what one person does, even if it's small, can make a difference in the lives of many."

CHAPTER 10

The Path of Compassion Is a Straight Path

It is written in the prophet Isaiah,

"See, I am sending my messenger ahead of you,
*   who will prepare your way;*
the voice of one crying out in the wilderness:
*   'Prepare the way of the Lord,*
*   make his paths straight',"*

John the baptizer appeared in the wilderness, proclaiming a baptism of repentance for the forgiveness of sins. And people from the whole Judean countryside and all the people of Jerusalem were going out to him, and were baptized by him in the river Jordan, confessing their sins. Now John was clothes with camel's hair, with a leather belt around his waist, and he ate locusts and wild honey. He proclaimed, "The one who is more powerful than I is coming after me; I am not worthy to stoop down and untie the thong of his sandals. I have baptized you with water; but he will baptize you with the Holy Spirit."

—Mark 1:2-8

Prayer

Gracious and loving God. There are no short-cuts through the trials. Keep us on the straight path that leads us home. Give us signs to point us in the right direction. And bless us with patience and hope all along the way. All for the sake of love. *Amen*.

Compassion Can Be a Hard Road

John the Baptist's prophetic cry in the desert wilderness is a call for us to live and serve with compassion. Before Jesus calls his disciples to the mountaintop to hear the words of discipleship, John the Baptist had already prepared the way for him. He was a prophet who lived the hard road of compassion. What John proclaimed, and how he lived, was the model for how we can be brave enough to serve with great courage and compassion. John, the descendant of the voice of the prophet Isaiah, calls out to all who have ears, "Make straight a pathway through the desert."

> "Your rod and your staff—they comfort me."
>
> **—Psalm 23:4**

I have only been lost in the desert once; it was about twenty-five years ago and once was enough. I went with a Botswanan friend, Tendani, who claimed to know the desert, so we headed off in a straight line toward our destination. We got picked up by a big ATV truck that drove us about ninety miles and dropped us off. In no time we realized we were completely lost. Fortunately, we found refuge from a nomadic group who gave us shelter and by the time we got out, *five days later*, my respect for the desert and gratitude for beds with linens was life changing. I learned that walking in a straight line doesn't mean you are on a straight path or even on your way to your destination. In the desert you can walk for days in a line, but you may not be getting a bit closer to home.

Isaiah first made that proclamation that Mark quotes from the desert wilderness of exile. Near the end of the Babylonian captivity in the sixth century B.C., he cries out to his people scattered and wounded about a promised land. He preaches that this promised land will be a place where the mountains will be made low, valleys will be raised up; where people, who are called by God's name and precious in God's sight, will go home. And he says that God will make a way out of no way. It was a message of hope and comfort for Isaiah's people, who had hung up their lyres and wept. He swore by the name of the Creator of heaven and earth who created them and never abandons those who mourn or suffer under the yoke of oppression.

Mark's Gospel begins with John the Baptist picking up Isaiah's song and calling the faithful back into the desert wilderness to remember who they are, where they are headed, and to prepare the way of the Lord. John was no one from nowhere, a soul not worthy to tie the shoes of the One coming; and yet it is his clear and prophetic voice that begins the proclamation of the Gospel. It is a powerful opening. It takes a strong and distinct voice to cut a straight path through the desert. It takes prophets with a clear vision of where they are headed, people who won't get sidetracked by dark nights, mirages, and fatigue. You keep going.

The principle of making a straight path in the desert bears out in mathematics as well. If two people pick two points on two lines close together, but the lines have different slopes, those two points could be miles apart. John's voice is strong and clear, just like Isaiah's. It served to cut through thick desert sand that burns cheeks and makes each step hard. It's a voice that gets our slopes realigned with the ethic of love rooted in the path of the gospel. It's a voice that is hard to hear. It wakes us up and asks us to stand at the banks of our Jordans and repent and realign our lives.

In Matthew's Gospel Jesus defends John with the words, "What then did you go out to see? Someone dressed in soft robes?" A voice crying in the wilderness is a unique voice—as wild and unadulterated as locust and honey. John doesn't mince words. He calls us to realign our paths so we can prepare our way for our Lord. He says loud and clear there is much suffering and brokenness in the world. As a whole community we need to repent and have compassion and bear fruit worthy of repentance.

Those are hard words to hear, but they were also hard to say. John was arrested and beheaded for speaking his truth. He wasn't even sure of his path—in Matthew when John is in prison he sends his disciples to Jesus. He is looking for reassurance—did I get it right, are you the one? Jesus answers by telling John's disciples to go back and report to John what they have seen. The poor have been brought great news. The lame have walked and the blind have seen. That is all the proof John needs.

"My help comes from the LORD, who made heaven and earth."

—Psalm 121:2

Compassion Prepares the Way

Here is why we love John—he is a prophet who is unafraid. When we get lost, his voice can echo in our hearts—crying out in the wilderness—come repent and remember we are unworthy to even stoop down and tie the shoe of the One who is coming. John is not bound by norms and institutions that would silence him. He helps us think deeply and live independently in our lives of faith. He is not afraid to call a community that has oppressed the captives, the most vulnerable, the widows, the refugees, the remnant of the Babylonian captivity to get them to get back in line with love's path. He reminds us to go back to the banks of our river Jordans. Think deeply. Speak our truth in love. Repent. Cry out so we can find our way through any desert. No one can do that for us. But do we have to find our way to the banks and back all by ourselves? No, we are not left orphaned. There is One who goes before us. Who leads us in the paths of righteousness. Who brings us to his house.

My son, Caney, is sixteen years old. He is a painter who teaches me through his art how one makes a straight path. He has a vision of what the painting will look like and he can render things quite closely—if an eye is not right, he reworks and keeps it on task to meet his vision. Undaunted, he can work ten hours on painting the back of a chair or an ankle. He never wavers. He is a true artist, a cousin to the prophet, because of it. Martin Luther King Jr. was also a descendant of John to be sure, and he used the words and metaphors of Isaiah with a painter's precision. In his famous "I Have a Dream" speech, he spoke of the vision and reminds us that the vision isn't ours to hold; it's a communal vision of the kingdom or the Blessed Community, as he called it. He said he had seen the Promised Land and that's where we were headed, and while he might not get there himself, we could, if we walk the path of love and compassion.

CHAPTER 11

Learning to Suffer With

When Jesus saw the crowds, he went up the mountain; and after he sat down, his disciples came to him. Then he began to speak, and taught them, saying:

"Blessed are the poor in spirit, for theirs is the kingdom of heaven.

"Blessed are those who mourn, for they will be comforted.

"Blessed are the meek, for they will inherit the earth.

"Blessed are those who hunger and thirst for righteousness, for they will be filled.

"Blessed are the merciful, for they will receive mercy.

"Blessed are the pure in heart, for they will see God.

"Blessed are the peacemakers, for they will be called children of God.

"Blessed are those who are persecuted for righteousness' sake, for theirs is the kingdom of heaven.

"Blessed are you when people revile you and persecute you and utter all kinds of evil against you falsely on my account. Rejoice and be glad, for your reward is great in heaven, for in the same way they persecuted the prophets who were before you."

—Matthew 5:1-12

Prayer

May the tears I have shed for others be a testimony to my love for you, my Lord. Let the path of mercy carry me closer to your heart and let me never turn back. Then guide me further and knit my will to you, so that I am wholly yours and dedicated to you. So that one day, I may perfectly love you. *Amen.*

Compassion Suffers With

Compassion literally means "to suffer with." I think some alternative definitions might include "to walk alongside," "to feel with," "to be open to," or "to love for." As a caregiver sitting by a bedside, you can sometimes literally feel all the people in the room. Everyone's eyes can be closed, and you can feel the sister praying, you can feel the mother holding on, you can feel the love. Even if the room is full of people unknown to you before this moment, you can feel compassion rising and the connection that all humanity shares in their grief.

There is something comforting about being familiar with the scene of hospice and what a body goes through to transition from this world. I saw a booklet at a hospital once that I thought was very compassionate. It talked about the four stages of dying in simple, straightforward ways. It is compassionate because it is truthful and takes the fear out of witnessing what many bodies have to go through in the last stages of death. I wish I had read that book when I began doing chaplaincy work. It is so much to take in, watching a person struggle with breathing and then seeing all the swelling around the hands and feet. There is a gift to realizing the process itself is normal—that doesn't mean it is not painful; it just means we don't have to be scared. It means that other people have walked through this valley before us and this holy wilderness has a path through it. The power of death can change us all and it can always be scary. The gift that caregivers and chaplains can offer is that we can make it a bit less fearful. The gift given to chaplains and caregivers is that it makes us a bit more faithful.

Compassion Is Faithful

In Matthew 5, Jesus begins teaching his disciples about what it means to do faithful ministry with a call to compassion. We call his teaching the Beatitudes. He says that even those who are suffering, mourning, and humbled by life are blessed. They are blessed by others' willingness to stand with them in their troubles, by God's presence, and by the place it opens in our hearts when we hurt. By beginning ministry with compassion, Jesus reminds us that compassion is a part of a generous love. Before a friend died last year after two years of illness, he said that experiencing the generosity of others was what had been the biggest blessing in his life. He wished he had known how to experience that before he got sick. In other words, he wished he had lived with more awareness about the gift of compassion before it was only part of his life as a patient.

"Though the fig tree does not blossom, and no fruit is on the vines;...yet I will rejoice in the LORD; I will exult in the God of my salvation."

—Habakkuk 3:17-18

We worship a faithful, compassionate God. One of the most beautiful prayers in the *Book of Common Prayer* says:

> O God, you made us in your own image and redeemed us through Jesus your Son: Look with compassion on the whole human family; take away the arrogance and hatred which infects our hearts; break down the walls that separate us; unite us in bonds of love; and work through our struggle and confusion to accomplish your purposes on earth; that, in your good time, all nations and races may serve you in harmony around your heavenly throne; through Jesus Christ our Lord. *Amen.*

God feels compassion for the whole world. It means that offering compassionate care is truly standing in the line of Moses and Jesus, and honoring the very heart of God.

The Beatitudes can carry us from the ordinary hardness of life into the extraordinary life found in a deep and abiding faith. It is in facing the ordinary burdens of suffering and death that we become holy and life-giving people. It is in those seasons that we bond as brothers and sisters, and form our capacity for compassion as we move from thinking of miracle cures to being a healing presence. It is the place where we can stand even at death's door with an abiding sense of God's presence in our lives. All we have to do is go back to the mountaintop, or to the river's edge, and be present. We don't have to pray the right prayer, say the right thing, or get it exactly right. Grace will make up the difference. We can simply show up and believe that in love we can find our way home.

We are following in a long line of compassionate saints and ministers who serve a compassionate God who loves the whole world. My work in serving the community of Magdalene and Thistle Farms and being a chaplain is like having a front-row seat to the daily miracle of love's healing power. I have seen hundreds of grieving families come and donate clothing from people they love who have died. They lay the treasure at the door, ready for it to be transformed into a gift for someone who needs it. I have sat in meetings and prayed for something we desperately need, and then within hours get a call or an e-mail, or run into a person who has just what we thought was out of reach. I have seen, in the midst of brokenness and suffering, the beauty of compassion rise up and cover everyone with healing.

We received our own distiller to process essential oils for healing at Thistle Farms. At the dedication of the still, we stood in a circle and prayed, "Almighty

God, we thank you for making us in your image. Revive the work of our hands in this place, now to be set apart for making healing oils, to help heal broken bodies and spirits, to give hope to women, to share the story of healing with the world, and to honor the donor and her appreciation of all living things." Out of the brokenness and healing of our donor, a beatitude was blooming, and it was fragrant and lovely. As we walk through a hurting world, it is good to carry the Beatitudes with us, to keep our hearts and minds open to all the blessings along the way.

The Beatitudes feel as though they were written in a language called compassion. There is enough space and dignity in the words to make the reader want to live with more compassion. We can imagine the crowd gathered, listening to Jesus speak these words, and the hearts of all the listeners turning to flesh as the words of blessedness are offered. There is a language of compassion. It is communicated in all kinds of ways as we care for those who are in crisis. The language is subtle and is about opening the space for other people to feel safe enough to be themselves.

> "To the weak I became weak, so that I might win the weak."
>
> **—1 Corinthians 9:22**

I used to run along Rock Creek Parkway in Maryland every evening after work at Bread for the World. It was a lonely year where I was growing in compassion as I learned about the issues of suffering in the world by the millions of people who are hungry. After I left work, I would put on my headphones and running shoes and head out for a run along the parkway. In my CD player, I kept playing a recording titled *Winter* by George Winston. The music was full of compassion, and what it did was open up a space in me where I could grieve the personal loneliness I was feeling as well as the global injustices that woke me up to the suffering of the world. The music itself was tender and I am so grateful to all the musicians and composers who offer music in that compassionate spirit.

Compassion Is Poetry

The language of compassion also includes silence, poetry, and sweet words that rise from our hearts as we try to tell someone that they are loved. All of those languages allow the grief in others, and in us, the dignity they deserve. Poetry in itself is a language born of a great compassion for the world. To write poetry one's heart as well as one's eyes must be wide open to the world around them, to what is stirring within them. A poet feels a moment with heart-wrenching clarity and tries to offer that gift to the reader to help them see that moment as a shared experience. Poetry comes from a space where colors are seen in real light from the perspective of a writer whose desire is to take in all the beauty and pain. Taking in the reality of life in all its colors does mean we are not afraid to experience pain. Poetry can draw us in like prayer and lift us to a new perspective and place. It seems to me that poetry is big enough for our searching hearts while we grieve and hold people up who are suffering. I think that old poetry is one of the best gifts a caregiver can take with them on the journey when we need to remember the language of compassion. I remember the first time I read the words of "Sweet Afton" by Robert Burns. The piece describes a river called Afton, in Ayrshire, Scotland, and was written in 1791. Since that time it has been made into lyrics for music and written on cards and letters by people who desire to express the language of belovedness. The words themselves flow like a gentle river:

> Flow gently, sweet Afton! amang
> thy green braes,
> Flow gently, I'll sing thee a song
> in thy praise;

My Mary's asleep by thy
murmuring stream,
Flow gently, sweet Afton, disturb
not her dream.

The words leave room for the mystery of life and death, of hope and loneliness, and of waking and dreaming. I believe that the language of compassion has to hold all of these elements in the balance.

> "Let us also lay aside every weight and the sin that clings so closely, and let us run with perseverance the race that is set before us."
> —**Hebrews 12:1**

Compassion Is the Best I Have to Offer

Finally, I think that sincerity and compassion walk side by side. What might seem like compassionate language coming from one person might seem contrived or like a platitude from another. My most sincere presence with someone is as unique as my preaching style or advice in a pastoral setting. It arises from a solid ground of prayer and contemplation. It is a blend of the lessons I have learned from other teachers and healers. It is the best I have to offer another.

O God, whose days are without end, and whose mercies cannot be numbered: Make us, we pray, deeply aware of the shortness and uncertainty of life; and let your Holy Spirit lead us in holiness and righteousness all our days; that, when we shall have served you in our generation, we may be gathered to our ancestors, having the testimony of a good conscience, in the communion of the Catholic Church, in the confidence of a certain faith, in the comfort of a religious and holy hope, in favor with you, our God, and in perfect charity with the world. All this we ask through Jesus Christ our Lord. *Amen*. (*The Book of Common Prayer,* "Burial II")

Eternal Spring

Spring in the Tennessee woods is a call to worship.
Tulip poplars usher in those who thirst for new life.
Carved hearts from old love in their bark become
signs to pilgrims.
A redbud arbor forms an aisle where new soft earth
Unfolds like a prayer rug.
Squirrels appear in haloed light slowing time.
Scurrying fawns in innocent tan coats remind the
weary to play.
Five thousand wildflowers on the hillside witness
That a handful of seeds can multiply like Gratitude
Spilling over a cup of grace.

In Tennessee spring all creation joins in the service.
Oils from the tree of life are a healing balm,
Falling like tears for those in pain.
Nature's prophets step up to preach for all the
passersby.
"There's a wheel in a wheel," says Ezekiel's vine
twisting in the sky.
"You shall be led out in peace," whispers Isaiah's
bloodroot.
Mountain laurel offers incense as sassafras clap
their hands.
The shale hill, like a snake, sheds a layer and is made

Low from the kiss of wind and rain.
The perfect circle of a spiderweb invites a joyful "Amen."

In Tennessee spring we are all reborn.
We sing the old songs with mourning doves and redbirds,
And join in the Alleluia chorus of the cicadas that drown our fears.
We lift our eyes to the hills where the elder oaks sway in delight.
Our wonder lets us enter the gates of thanksgiving with praise
Proclaiming the goodness of our Creator.
A rising creek, like a closing prayer, carries us
To the banks of Amos's vision of a river of justice.
We are weak in the knees thinking this piece of heaven
Will be lost too soon in kudzu vines or drought,
Until we hear a barred owl's echo from Eden's hollow
Reminding us there is a deep, eternal spring that never lets us go.

—becca stevens